SECONDARY TEACHER'S
Pocketbook

2nd Edition

By Brin Best

Cartoons:
Phil Hailstone

Published by:

Teachers' Pocketbooks
Laurel House, Station Approach,
Alresford, Hampshire SO24 9JH, UK
Tel: +44 (0)1962 735573
Fax: +44 (0)1962 733637
E-mail: sales@teacherspocketbooks.co.uk
Website: www.teacherspocketbooks.co.uk

*Teachers' Pocketbooks is an imprint of
Management Pocketbooks Ltd.*

© Brin Best 2003 and 2008

First edition published 2003. Reprinted 2005.

First Edition 2003 ISBN 978 1 903776 50 6
This Edition 2008 ISBN 978 1 903776 88 9

British Library Cataloguing-in-Publication
Data – A catalogue record for this book is
available from the British Library.

Design, typesetting and graphics by Efex Ltd.
Printed in UK.

Contents

How to use this Pocketboook

This Pocketbook is designed to be an everyday companion for teachers working in secondary schools. The accessible style and use of bullet points mean you can read the whole book in a couple of hours, or as a busy teacher keep it handy for future reference and dip into relevant sections when you have a spare five minutes.

As we find out more about the brain and how people learn, the craft of teaching is undergoing something of a revolution. Teachers are beginning to get spectacular results by using a range of new approaches that motivate their students and help them learn. This book condenses key insights, ideas and advice. It can be used:

- As a source of **ideas** and **strategies** to help you improve your teaching
- To encourage you to **reflect** on your professional practice
- To stimulate **discussion** among your colleagues
- To help you **progress** in your career
- As a handy **reference** to key educational issues

However you use the book, I hope it will prove useful to you in developing your teaching skills and becoming a more effective and reflective practitioner.

Preparing
to Teach

 The Craft
of Teaching

 Other Aspects
of the Role

 Progressing in
Your Career

 Reference
Section

 Further
Information

Preparing
to Teach

What is teaching? What is learning?

Teaching can be viewed as any purposeful action designed to bring about a learning gain in an individual or group. It is your main role as a teacher to help your students learn, but what does *learning* actually mean?

Learning is a change in pupils' behaviour which takes place as a result of being engaged in an educational experience
Kyriacou 1997

In thinking about the types of learning taking place in your classroom, consider the following ways in which learning can be demonstrated (after Gagné):

- **Intellectual skills –** demonstrating concepts, applying rules and solving problems

- **Verbal skills**
- **Cognitive (mental) strategies –** applied to learning

- **Attitudes**
- **Motor skills**

As you teach be aware how students are demonstrating their learning, to what degree and the types of teaching approaches that promote them. Consider how well individual students are learning and what individuals' barriers to learning might be.

In the twentieth century two psychologists' ideas about learning proved very influential: Jean Piaget and Lev Vygotsky.

Piaget: cognitive development

Swiss psychologist Jean Piaget (1896-1980) suggested children go through a series of **stages** in their cognitive (intellectual) development, each with characteristic modes of thought. He argued that children must pass through these stages before they construct the ability to perceive, reason and understand in mature and rational terms. He believed that the development of intelligence was the result of dynamic **interaction between the child and the environment** and that:

- Children's thinking is different from mature adults'
- All children develop through the same sequence of stages
- Children's thinking at each stage is different from that at other stages
- Cognitive development is not a continuous accumulation of things learnt, instead *intellectual revolutions* change the structure of intelligence

Proponents of this theory believed that active, **experiential learning** should be encouraged in the classroom as this provides the optimum conditions to promote pupils' natural capacity to develop and learn.

Vygotsky: social constructivist theory

Russian philosopher and psychologist Lev Vygotsky (1896-1934) shared some important areas of agreement with Piaget. But he differed in his emphasis on the importance of **instruction and language** in promoting learning and developing intelligence.

The theory, which was further adapted by Jerome Bruner (1915-), maintained that:

- There are important relationships between language and thinking
- Communication, social interaction and instruction are vital
- Learning involves the search for patterns and predictability
- A zone of proximal development exists for an individual, this being the gap between what that individual can do on their own and what they can achieve when aided by a more knowledgeable or skilled person

Those who favoured this theory stressed that **guided discovery learning** should be used in the classroom, where teachers use much verbal prompting to develop learning.

Information-processing theory

Towards the end of the twentieth century a number of education psychologists proposed the **information-processing theory**, which was influenced by the ideas of both Piaget and Vygotsky, but also had its own distinctive philosophy.

This theory emphasises cognitive **strategies** rather than structures and maintains that:

- Fundamental processes and strategies underpin all cognitive activity
- The brain processes information relating to perception, problem-solving and memory in the short-term memory, but stores it as abstractions in the long-term memory
- The processes are the same for all individuals but speed and efficiency vary from one learner to another
- Cognitive development is the process of learning more and gaining helpful strategies to analyse, remember and problem-solve

The main implications for the classroom of the information-processing theory are that **concrete examples and experiences are important** in developing abstractions, and instruction is key to developing appropriate strategies.

Educational theories in the classroom

As a teacher it is important that you are aware of the main theories relating to how children learn. They provide you with a framework to analyse learning situations and a language to describe the learning taking place in your classroom.

Practical tips:

- Try to develop a **repertoire** of teaching styles and approaches, and then see how each works with a particular lesson, or a specific class
- Adopt an **experimental** and **reflective** approach to your teaching, where you try things out and evaluate their success
- Remember that each teaching strategy you use has the **potential** to promote learning – the degree to which it actually does this in a particular lesson may be beyond your control

> *Every challenge you overcome makes you a stronger and better person*
> **Paula Radcliffe**

New approaches to teaching and learning

As we learn more about how children learn from research into the brain, new ideas are being introduced into schools. This can be threatening to some teachers who have always taught in a particular way, or feel they have *heard it all before* and the so-called new ideas will *go out of fashion* again.

Although some of the newer approaches being recommended do have parallels with the teaching of the liberal 1960s and 1970s, the difference is **we now have scientific evidence to back them up**. Things have come full circle and what felt right for many teachers in the past can now be backed up by hard data.

Brain research and teaching

We should pay close attention to research on the brain and the implications for teaching and learning because effective teaching is intrinsically linked to the functioning of the brain.

Your brain is like a sleeping giant **Tony Buzan**

Did you know?

- The brain is the most complicated organ known in the universe and we only understand a few aspects of how it works
- The science of the brain and learning is very young and new discoveries are being made every year

Remember that

- Professionals in other fields (eg medicine) readily adapt their practice in the light of new scientific discoveries, so why should teaching be any different?
- Change is inevitable and we have to adapt to it rather than being a victim of it

Learning styles 1

There has been a huge upsurge in interest in the study of **learning styles** in recent years. Learners can be categorised as mainly:

 Visual – Approximately 29% of people have a visual learning preference.

 Auditory – Approximately 34% of people have an auditory learning preference.

 Kinaesthetic – Approximately 37% of people have a kinaesthetic learning preference.

It is important not to categorise any individual as **solely** a visual, auditory or kinaesthetic learner. They have a **preferred** or habitual learning style which tends to dominate.

Learning styles 2

Learners tend to process information in one of two ways:

Wholists – they process information in wholes
Analysts – they process information in parts

A key challenge for a teacher is to ensure that learners of all types are included in learning experiences, while at the same time encouraging individuals to develop their learning skills in areas which may not come naturally to them.

Learning **strategies** on the other hand are less fixed, and refer to the techniques your students select to tackle a particular task.

Multiple intelligences

The Harvard University professor Howard Gardner revolutionised our view of intelligence in the late 1980s with his theory of **multiple intelligences**. According to Gardner's work there are eight different intelligences:

- **Interpersonal** – for communicating with others
- **Intrapersonal** – for self-discovery and analysis
- **Linguistic** – for reading, writing and speech
- **Mathematical/logical** – for maths, logic and systems
- **Visual/spatial** – for visualisation and art
- **Bodily-kinaesthetic** – for touch and reflex
- **Musical** – for rhythm and music
- **Naturalist** – for studying and classifying the natural world

Multiple intelligences

Everybody possesses the eight intelligences to some extent, but we all have particular strengths. Schools have enthusiastically embraced the theory because it gets away from the narrow notion of **intelligence quotient (IQ)**. Every student in your class is intelligent in at least one way!

You can carry out **questionnaires** with your students to check their preferred learning style and determine their intelligence profile. They give you extremely valuable information to help you plan appropriate learning experiences.

Excellent **internet links** to education websites on learning styles and multiple intelligences, including various diagnostic questionnaires, can be found at www.support4learning.org.uk. Smith (1998) also contains some useful questionnaires.

However, be wary of labelling and pigeon-holing students on the basis of any of these questionnaires. Treat them as useful for gathering information about individual learners, but remember preferences are not fixed and we should try to extend learners as much as possible.

If we insist on looking at the rainbow of intelligence through a single filter, many minds will erroneously seem devoid of light
Renée Fuller

Accelerated learning

In the last few years there has been an enthusiastic uptake by teachers of so-called **accelerated learning** methods. Much of this has resulted from the efforts of inspirational trainers such as Alistair Smith, who have written some very influential books in this area.

- Accelerated learning is an approach to teaching that takes account of recent knowledge research on the brain and learning
- It marries this with some theories, only some of which have research evidence to back them up, but which are popular with teachers
- Several schools using the methods have received excellent Ofsted inspection reports for the quality of teaching and learning
- The pace of change within this field is relentless as new information on the brain floods into the scientific and educational literature

Accelerated learning is now firmly embedded as an essential element of effective teaching and learning in many schools. Teachers are discovering it is a very effective way to re-engage students in learning and raise levels of motivation. *The Accelerated Learning Pocketbook* gives extensive information on how to introduce the methods into your classroom.

Accelerated learning in a nutshell

Here is the 'big picture' showing you how to create an accelerated learning lesson:

1. Ensure your students are in the correct **physical state** to learn (proper hydration and nourishment are important, as are room temperature and oxygen levels)

2. Use **music in a structured way** (see page 64-5)

3. Help students enter a positive **emotional state** for learning

4. Create an **environment that supports learning** but make activities challenging

5. Develop **good working relationships** with your students and use praise frequently

6. Plan **inclusive learning activities** that respect the full range of learning styles and intelligences, and are **accessible** to all students

Accelerated learning in a nutshell (cont'd)

7. Include this **sequence** in lessons (see pages 37-39 for details):
   Part 1: put the learning in context   Part 2: starter
   Part 3: main teaching and learning   Part 4: plenary

8. Allow **breaks** for light physical activity

9. Use a **variety of teaching methods**, including thinking skills and visual tools to develop higher order skills

10. Make **learning skills** such as mind-mapping and memory techniques part of your lesson

11. Encourage students to **review** their own progress and set personal goals

12. **Evaluate** your lesson in consultation with your students

It is vital to appreciate that the most effective learning occurs when **all**, or as many as possible, of these elements are **combined** in your lessons. Simply turning on music or getting students to drink water or draw mind maps will not result in accelerated learning in itself, and you must place great emphasis on the actual **teaching strategies** you use in your lessons.

Developing your own pedagogy

There are still devotees in the educational world to the ideas of Piaget and Vygotsky. But to take one side or the other in designing your lessons would be to miss the point. Both schools of thought, along with the more recent ideas on how children learn, have something to offer by way of helping us understand the complexity of teaching.

- A large amount of research has been carried out in the last few decades into learning theory and effective teaching methods
- It is not possible to give a list of everything you need to do to ensure that your students learn effectively, quite simply because we do not know all the answers yet
- The summary of recent research findings on the next page outlines some fundamental principles that are now widely accepted by experts on learning
- These ideas help you to develop your own distinctive **pedagogy** of teaching, that will change and develop as you gain in experience

What research evidence shows

Research has shown that the following factors are important in designing
effective learning experiences:

1. **Relate** any new learning to what is already known by your students
2. Your students will learn more and remember better if information has been taught
   and learned according to a **coherent structure** – ie give them the big picture first
3. Concepts are more easily grasped when your students are introduced to new ideas via
   concrete examples and given opportunities to compare and contrast new stimuli
4. Learning is more effective where your students are **actively involved** in the learning
   process through critical thinking, discussion and awareness of their own learning
   strategies
5. Your role in structuring learning experiences is critical – **instruction should be
   facilitative and interventionist**, with transmission methods (eg copying) rarely used
6. **Develop a variety of teaching methods**, ways of presenting information, resources
   and assessment methods to enhance opportunities for your students to use their
   habitual learning styles and learning strategies
7. **Other factors** such as self-esteem, motivation, peer pressure and social grouping can
   have an effect on learning

Adapted from Capel *et al*. (1999)

Schemes of work

Your **schemes of work** should outline the knowledge, skills and understanding that you wish your students to gain from a particular unit of work. Schemes of work:

- Are the responsibility of the head of department but you should have a role in shaping them
- Should have the input of all members of a department
- Are usually written in tabular form – headings should include Key questions, Activities, Resources, ICT opportunities, Assessment opportunities
- Should be regularly revised
- Need to take account of changes in syllabuses and new government initiatives

Lesson planning

Good **lesson plans** are the foundation of effective teaching. Lesson planning takes a long time, especially in the early stages of your career. It becomes quicker with experience. Make sure your lesson plans:

- Include learning outcomes, activities, timings, resources, homework and lesson evaluation
- Include extension activities for students who complete work earlier than expected
- Are concise and easy to read

In some schools you are required to submit your lesson plans to the headteacher a week in advance – a sure way to focus the mind!

Experienced teachers sometimes claim they do not prepare lesson plans. In reality they do prepare them **mentally**, even if they do not record them on paper. It has become so automatic this no longer seems necessary – until the Ofsted inspectors arrive!

Embracing new initiatives

Schools are being bombarded with a range of new initiatives and teachers can sometimes feel overwhelmed by the pace of change.

Thinking skills guru Dr Robert Fisher says that in implementing any new teaching and learning initiatives into your school remember that the **unit of change** is the lesson. Do not try to change everything you do at once.

If you can incorporate a new idea or approach into just one lesson then you have made a start. Have the confidence and enthusiasm to keep experimenting.

The journey of a thousand miles begins with a single step
Chinese proverb

Tools of the trade

You should assemble a **teacher's toolkit** that accompanies you into every classroom:

- Chalk in various colours and/or whiteboard markers
- A small box of spare equipment for students to borrow (pens, pencils, rulers)
- A pad of plain white paper for planning, demonstrating, showing examples

These are timeless hands-on tools that complement any electronic equipment in your classroom. Other essentials include:

- Your teacher planner and mark book
- A bottle of water to stay hydrated
- *The Secondary Teacher's Pocketbook* for reference, ideas and inspiration!

Dress code and appearance

How you present yourself can have an important influence on your students and their parents/carers. Students often take a real interest in how their teachers dress – new shoes, a Christmas pair of socks, the fresh hair cut all tend to get noticed and remarked upon!

Although how you choose to dress depends partly on the subject you teach, be mindful of the messages your dress sends out. **Try to put over a smart, professional appearance** and pay attention to the details – your hair, nails and state of your shoes. It is surprising how these make a difference to how people judge you. Would you want to be seen by a scruffy, unkempt doctor or dentist?

The classroom environment

Classrooms should be stimulating multi-sensory environments where learning is fun. **A number of recent studies have linked increased motivation and achievement with stimulating classroom environments.** Historically, secondary schools paid less attention to environment than primaries, with their superb displays, colourful artefacts and every space used to celebrate or stimulate.

In recent years most secondary schools have gone a long way to improving their classroom environments and see this as an integral part of teaching and learning.

A stimulating classroom environment

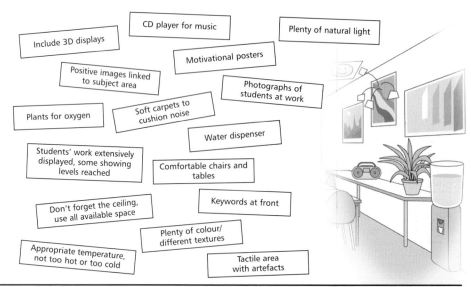

Include 3D displays

CD player for music

Plenty of natural light

Motivational posters

Positive images linked to subject area

Photographs of students at work

Plants for oxygen

Soft carpets to cushion noise

Water dispenser

Students' work extensively displayed, some showing levels reached

Comfortable chairs and tables

Don't forget the ceiling, use all available space

Keywords at front

Plenty of colour/ different textures

Appropriate temperature, not too hot or too cold

Tactile area with artefacts

Preparing
to Teach

 The Craft
of Teaching

 Other Aspects
of the Role

 Progressing in
Your Career

 Reference
Section

 Further
Information

The Craft of Teaching

Classroom rules

You should come up with a simple set of **classroom rules** in collaboration with your students. These will be a common point of reference for everyone. The aim of classroom rules is to outline the behaviour that will result in a **purposeful** and **supportive** working atmosphere for everyone – to create a classroom where the **focus is on learning**.

- The most powerful way to establish these rules is to ask your students to help devise them during their first lesson with you
- Contrary to what some teachers think, students are usually surprisingly sensible and practical when asked to identify such rules – they are also much more likely to keep to them if they have been involved in drawing them up

If you make it clear that poor behaviour is simply not a feature of your classroom, your students will soon get used to that – but you have to actively manage and cultivate that atmosphere. Having high expectations at all times will pre-empt many instances of poor behaviour.

Classroom rules – a step-by-step approach

1. Ask students to write down on separate Post-it notes (or pieces of paper) what they can do to ensure a good working atmosphere in lessons

2. Using a different colour Post-it note ask them to write down the things that others do in lessons that make it difficult for them to learn

3. On two areas of the board ask each student to come up and place their ideas in turn, reading them out as they do so

4. Discuss the ideas that have been suggested. There will be many areas of overlap which can be clustered. Address any inappropriate responses

5. Ask the group to draw up a simple statement that summarises each cluster

6. Print the agreed rules onto A3 sheets, laminate them and display in your classroom

7. Get each student to write the agreed rules in the back of their exercise books

An excellent classroom tool, *The LVT thinking skills kit*, can be used as a more robust alternative to Post-it notes. Read about it at www.logovisual.com/education/.

Example of classroom rules

This is a learning classroom

1. We will respect other people, their opinions and property

2. We will try our best

3. We will help others, especially when they are stuck

4. We will not talk when other people are talking to the class

5. We will work safely and sensibly

Your most valuable asset in learning is a positive attitude
Bobbi DePorter

> Take care with your friends' equipment. People who nick each others' stuff are a pain. Respect what others have to say. Make each other feel welcome.

> Always try hard. I don't like it when people put you down when you are trying hard. Be positive about your work. Co-operate with others.

> Appreciate other people's difficulties. It's annoying when people don't help you when you find work hard. Help each other with work. Be friendly.

> Learn when to be silent. People who are rude when I answer a question are mean. Be silent when necessary. Put your hand up if you want to say something.

> Take care with machines. Be safe. People are a pain when they mess around with dangerous things in class.

Rules for the teacher

Give your students the chance to say **what they expect of a teacher too**.
This is ideally done in the lesson after they have set the ground rules for their own behaviour in lessons. Once again, the results they give you will almost always be very sensible and useful.

- Use the same method as for the classroom rules activity, but with each student writing down the things that teachers do that help or hinder learning
- This will give you an insight into what students understand by effective teaching – it will also indicate any sensitivities of particular students
- Do not be surprised if your students come up with the very same qualities you would expect in a teacher – they are very good judges of what they need to help them learn!
- You may want to share with the class what you think a really good teacher should be like – this could stimulate some interesting discussion

An excellent book by Ruddock and Flutter (See page 124) shows how students' views can be used to improve all aspects of school life.

Rules for the teacher (cont'd)

- Obviously there may be a few things your students suggest that are unrealistic or inappropriate, and you will need to address these with the class
- Let your students know you will record all their comments and try your best to be a really good teacher – but remind them that they can help you teach well by keeping to their rules too
- Let your students know that you will be asking for their comments throughout the year to help you become a better teacher (see *Ask your students how to improve* p75)

Students really appreciate the opportunity to give their views in this way, and it demonstrates as soon as you begin teaching them that:

- Their views matter to you
- You too are a learner in the classroom

Qualities of effective teachers

My own research has repeatedly shown that as far as young people are concerned the most **effective teachers** share six common qualities. They are:

1. Good at explaining things
2. Knowledgeable about their subject
3. Able to vary their teaching style
4. Friendly, approachable and have a sense of humour
5. Firm but fair
6. Genuinely interested in the progress of students

Academic studies of effective teachers build on the views of young people. Teachers judged to be effective:

- Establish orderly and attractive learning environments
- Maximise learning time and maintain an academic emphasis
- Deliver well-organised and well-structured lessons, with a clarity of purpose
- Convey high expectations and provide intellectual challenge
- Monitor progress and provide quick corrective feedback
- Establish clear and fair discipline

Based on Kyriacou (1988)

The classroom layout

Experiment with various **classroom layouts** to see the impact they have on your teaching methods and the group interaction that results from them.

The most suitable format for most teaching settings in school is where desks are arranged in a **horseshoe**. This works well because it:

- Allows maximum interaction between students
- Permits easy access to all students for the teacher
- Ensures the teacher can see all students' faces at all times

The **grouped table** is also useful, especially for collaborative work, but make sure students do not have their backs to you.

Some classrooms are obviously easier to rearrange than others (eg science labs). In these cases be creative with where students sit; for instance in group discussions or demonstrations at the front of the class, allow students to bring their stools with them.

Structuring a lesson

It is vital that you provide an **effective structure** for all your lessons that promotes learning. The one below is adapted from the four-part lesson structure outlined in the **Key Stage 3** strategy.

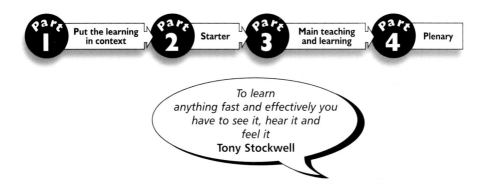

Part 1	Part 2	Part 3	Part 4
Put the learning in context	Starter	Main teaching and learning	Plenary

> *To learn anything fast and effectively you have to see it, hear it and feel it*
> **Tony Stockwell**

Structuring a lesson

It is important to provide an effective structure for all your lessons that promotes your students' learning. The following provides a 'brain-friendly' structure for your lessons.

Part 1: put the learning in context (about 5% of lesson time)
- Explore what the students learnt in the previous lesson
- Relate the learning to the overall syllabus
- Make the learning outcomes clear
- Explain what is coming in the next lesson
- Mind maps can be a very useful visual tool for this part of the lesson, showing students how an individual lesson fits into the wider course they are studying

Part 2: starter (about 10% of lesson time)
- Begin with a short activity which engages students' interest – a prop, story, exciting stimulus material
- Try to activate students' prior knowledge
- Prepare the students for the main teaching and learning that will follow

Structuring a lesson

Part 3: main teaching and learning (about 75% of lesson time)
- Students should be carrying out activities for as much of this time as possible
- You should act as a facilitator for their learning – try not to talk for too long
- Students should be engaged in multi-sensory learning that respects their learning styles and intelligence profiles, while also extending them in new ways
- All students should be set work which is of an appropriate level of challenge
- Allow choice over how students carry out tasks
- Learning should be broken down into achievable chunks
- Find plenty of opportunities to develop thinking skills

Part 4: plenary (about 10% of lesson time)
- Provides an opportunity for learning to be reviewed
- Students should be given the chance to reflect on what they think the main learning points of the lesson have been
- You should include careful use of teacher questioning (see page 47)

Before the lesson begins

Beginning the lesson in an appropriate way is very important as it sets the tone for the whole learning experience. Make sure you:

- **Arrive before the students** to give time for setting up
- **Greet each student** in a friendly and positive way
- **Insist students enter quietly** and settle down at their desks in an orderly manner
- **Set out the learning objectives** for the lesson on the board
- **Try to engage your students' interest** with a question or puzzle on the board

Beginning the teaching

Once parts 1 and 2 of the lesson are over, the initial segment of part 3, the main teaching and learning, should focus on the essential **input** to allow your students to carry out tasks that will embed learning. This can be done through:

- Teacher talk
- Reading, watching or listening to some stimulus material
- Questions and answers

During this part of the lesson **do not talk for too long**. The attention span of young people can be very short and long periods of teacher talk are not very engaging unless you are a particularly entertaining speaker.

You may need to deliver further input later in the lesson, but do not keep stopping students to make minor points.

Setting student tasks

Time when students are carrying out **tasks** should form the bulk of the lesson. You should aim to design activities that keep students engaged in their work for the maximum time possible. Essential points for this phase of the lesson are:

- Always give the tasks verbally **and** in writing to include different types of learners
- **Make sure that all students understand** what they have to do
- If you say, *'Put your hand up if you are not sure what I want you to do,'* you can judge whether you need to rephrase the tasks for the whole class, or if certain individuals need further support
- **Tasks should be carefully differentiated** to ensure all students can achieve success

Setting student tasks (cont'd)

- **Give a time frame** for the tasks, eg *'You have about 15 minutes to complete these questions, I'll stop you at 12 o'clock to see how things are going'*
- **Circulate widely** as students are working to check they are on task, progressing well and getting the appropriate responses
- **Do not insist that students work in silence** as long as their talk is focused on the tasks
- Where possible **offer choice** in the tasks undertaken or the way the results are presented
- **Include a wide variety of tasks** that appeal to different types of learners and different intelligences
- **Allow plenty of opportunity for pair work and group work** as well as individual work

Showing what students have learnt

It is important to give your students opportunities to **show what they have learnt**:

- By **checking** their own written responses
- By **reading out** their responses to others for discussion
- By giving **presentations** to the class
- By **completing** tests, quizzes and mind maps

One of your main roles as teacher, of course, is to **check and mark** students' written demonstration of their knowledge. This also gives the essential information you need on how they are progressing.

Feedback is one of the most important factors in helping students to learn, so think carefully about the kind of feedback you provide.

Teachers are being asked to think more carefully about the feedback they provide to learners as part of the Assessment for Learning approach. The key message is that learners need to be enabled to make better progress as they work, rather than simply being given a final mark once their work is complete.

The importance of review

It is important to provide opportunities for students to **review** what they have learnt. This is often done at the end of a lesson, but it is also useful to build in review opportunities into other parts of the lesson, or as homework tasks. Ways to review include:

- Writing out summary points
- Drawing a mind map of a lesson or topic
- Naming the most important thing learnt from a lesson
- Preparing flashcards or summary diagrams

Review is also an essential element of **revision** for tests and formal examinations.

Make sure that the **plenary** at the end of every lesson includes an activity which sums up what has been learnt and prepares students for the next lesson.

Pace of lessons

The **pace** of your lessons is important and this aspect frequently comes under scrutiny when you are inspected by Ofsted.

A lesson is well paced when:

- There is a **purposeful working atmosphere** with students encouraged to progress through tasks of increasing complexity
- New information is introduced only **when students are ready** to receive it
- **Tasks are challenging** and keep students engaged in their work
- **Students are clear** what they should be doing
- **It has a good momentum** that minimises opportunities for lulls

Do not confuse the pace of **learning** with the pace of **content**. It is easy to swamp students with information which hinders learning.

Questioning

A large chunk of your teacher talk should involve **questioning**. It helps you determine how much your students have understood and can lead on to higher level thinking skills.

Points to bear in mind about questioning:
- Use a **range** of questioning techniques
- Pitch the **language** and **content level** of questions appropriately
- Ask as many **open** questions as possible (see examples)
- **Prompt** and **give clues** where necessary
- Allow **thinking time** (at least five seconds for more complex questions)
- **Invite answers** from particular individuals as well as asking the whole class
- **Do not favour** students with higher ability or according to where they are seated (you will tend to neglect those closest to you and those right at the back of the room)
- Encourage students to **devise their own questions**

The only dumb question is a question you don't ask
Paul MacCready

Questioning

Open questions

Why did the second world war start?

Some people have said drugs should be legalised – why do you think they believe this?

To what extent do you think she was correct in carrying that out?

Closed questions

Did Hitler cause the second world war?

Should drugs be legalised?

Was she right or wrong?

Pair work

Students like working in pairs and **pair work** has tremendous educational value. It should be firmly established in the repertoire of every teacher.

Pair work has many uses, including:

- Exchanging and exploring ideas
- Checking understanding
- Conducting collaborative projects

Ground rules for pair work:

- Every student must be prepared to work with anybody else in the class
- Each person must listen carefully to the other
- **Disagreements** are permitted but **arguments** are not allowed
- Students of different ability can be paired together
- In collaborative projects the distribution of work must be fair
- If one of the pair breaks the rules they may be asked to work on their own

Group work

Group work can be a very enjoyable and productive way for students to learn. The main uses for group work are:

- Preparing a joint project
- Working on a presentation
- Discussing an issue

The ground rules for group work are similar to those for pair work. It is easier for students not to pull their weight when working with a larger group, so this needs to be carefully monitored.

Equally, it is important not to let the same students take the lead all the time – some students thrive on this, but others need to be allowed to take their turn.

Inclusion

Inclusion is a process in which you grasp every opportunity to ensure that each student reaches his/her potential. Your school should have an overarching inclusion policy which addresses the needs of all student groups.

There will be students in your classes who need specific help to overcome their barriers to learning. Such students may or may not have a statement of special educational need. They include students with:

- A learning disability
- A physical disability
- A mental disability
- A sensory impairment
- An emotional or behavioural difficulty

You will also teach students who are exceptionally **able** and need specially designed lessons to challenge them.

A teacher who is inclusive in their teaching will seek to include all these students, as well as responding to the individual needs, culture and values of the others in the class.

Eight steps to an inclusive classroom

1. Be aware of those students who have **barriers** to their learning, such as students with statements of special educational need
2. **Understand** what these barriers are and **what you can do to help** individuals overcome them
3. Bring in **support staff** to help individuals whose barriers to learning are particularly severe
4. Be aware of the **ability profile** of your students, including those who are very able
5. Be aware of the preferred **learning styles** of your students and their different **intelligences**
6. Be aware of the **culture** and **values** of the students in your class
7. **Plan lessons that will include all the students** in your class, ensuring work is of the appropriate level and is presented in an accessible and engaging way
8. **Monitor** how inclusive your teaching is by analysing whether all students and particular groups are making satisfactory progress, using this information to plan appropriate programmes and next steps

Effective differentiation

Differentiation involves adapting work and the way it is set in order to meet the needs of all students in your class. It is especially necessary in mixed-ability groups.

There are several types of differentiation:
1. **By task** – students cover the same content, but at different levels and with appropriate scaffolding to ensure successful outcomes
2. **By outcome** – the same general task is set, but students work through it at their own level, using recording methods appropriate to their needs
3. **By learning activity** – students work on the same task at the same level, but in a different way
4. **By pace** – students cover the same content at the same level, but at a different rate
5. **By dialogue** – where the teacher discusses the work with individual students to tailor the work to their needs

It is essential to differentiate work so that it is accessible to every student in your class, otherwise they will not learn effectively.

Adapted from Kyriacou (1998)

Working with very able pupils

In recent years there has been increasing emphasis on meeting the needs of students who are very able. According to the DCSF:

- Gifted and talented students are those who achieve, or have the ability to achieve, **significantly above average** for a student in their year group at their school
- **Gifted** students are defined as those with high ability in one or more of the National Curriculum subjects, other than art, PE, music or drama
- **Talented** students are defined as those with high ability in practical areas such as art, PE, music or drama
- Schools should identify **5-10% of each year group** as gifted and talented

Working with very able pupils

Guidelines for working with very able pupils:

- Be clear about **how many** very able (gifted and talented) students are in your classes
- Keep a register of the most able students in each class you teach
- Be aware of their **individual** strengths and weaknesses
- **Individual target-setting** can be an effective way of encouraging able pupils to reach their potential
- Make sure you design lessons that challenge and motivate very able students, as you would all the students in your class
- Offer enrichment activities, both on site and to external venues such as universities, museums and art galleries

Working with very able pupils

Characteristics of a lesson more likely to promote learning for very able pupils:

- Work is set at the **appropriate level** so that no-one is bored or finishes early
- It promotes **higher level** thinking skills
- Students work through an **enquiry** route rather than a series of unstructured tasks, especially where students are involved in setting the questions themselves
- Learning is **active** and encourages students to include their **own** experiences
- Extension tasks give scope for **originality** on both execution and presentation
- It encourages students to ask **questions**
- Students are encouraged to **evaluate** their work and suggest areas for improvement
- Teacher encourages students to **share** gifts or talents with the rest of class
- It promotes **ambiguity** and stresses that there are not always 'right' answers
- It values the **independence** of learners as they work, while providing enough support to ensure they are not abandoned and still feel 'safe' in the classroom

Maintaining classroom discipline

How to maintain the classroom discipline necessary for effective learning is an issue uppermost in the minds of most teachers. There is no secret formula to achieving good discipline.

- **Teachers have a range of approaches that can work** – softly spoken or booming, strict or more liberal
- Maintaining consistently **high expectations** is very important, as is the concept of learners having choices
- **A clear set of agreed classroom rules and consistent application of sanctions** if things go wrong underpin good behaviour (see pages 30-32 for more information)
- **Accept that you will encounter inappropriate behaviour**, and occasionally outright defiance, and concentrate on how to deal with each situation in the calmest way possible
- **Use a range of strategies** to pre-empt misbehaviour. Encourage students to see that they have **choices** over their behaviour and that they must take **responsibility** for these choices

If things are frequently going wrong with the whole class, or several members of it, seek the assistance of a senior member of staff to explore what is happening. **Make a plan, be determined and stick to it**.

Maintaining classroom discipline

Strategies to pre-empt inappropriate behaviour:

- Scan the classroom
- Circulate
- Make eye contact
- Target your questions
- Use proximity
- Give academic help
- Change activities or pace
- Notice misbehaviour
- Notice disrespect
- Move students

The *Behaviour Management Pocketbook*
provides a wealth of practical advice
on strategies to promote good
classroom discipline

Maintaining classroom discipline

What to do when things go wrong in your dealings with an individual

- **Do not take it personally** – there is usually a reason for the inappropriate behaviour and it is very rarely to do with you
- Criticise the **behaviour** not the **individual** – a bad act does not make a bad person
- Give **private** rather than public reprimands
- Be **firm** but avoid letting the situation **escalate**
- Remind the students of the **classroom rules**
- **Always give the student a way of saving face** – eg *'You can either move from your place now or we will take things further after the lesson'*
- Never issue personal **put downs**, even if the student is abusive
- Try not to get **angry** – this is the reaction the student sometimes wants to see
- Give plenty of opportunity for **fresh starts**
- Use **punishments** sparingly, in proportion to the *crime* and in line with school policy
- **Call for help** from a more senior member of staff if you feel things are getting out of control

Using sanctions and rewards

Good order in lessons can be helped by having a clear policy on **sanctions** and **rewards**, preferably at the whole school level.

Sanctions

- Should be used sparingly
- Must be applied fairly and consistently
- Should not denigrate or humiliate students
- Should be purposeful
- Should never be extra work or lines (extra learning should be a reward not a sanction!)

Rewards

- Should be given for effort as well as attainment
- Should not routinely be given for the same thing: this devalues them and can lead to students taking pleasure in the reward not the learning
- Should not be given so frequently that they become devalued
- Should be shared with parents/carers whenever possible
- Should be given in a way that does not embarrass the student

Do not confuse rewards with **praise** which should be given whenever possible and not as a special treat!

Resources for learning

Ensure that you use a really wide variety of stimulating **resources** to help your students learn. Use the checklist below to help ring the changes:

Over the last half-term which of the following resources have you used?

Television	❏	Newspaper article	❏
Video/DVD	❏	Website	❏
Computer	❏	Leaflet	❏
Camcorder	❏	Map	❏
Audio cassette player	❏	Aerial photograph	❏
Text book	❏	CD-ROM	❏
Non-fiction book	❏	Audio CD	❏
Fiction book	❏	Scientific equipment	❏

Varying your teaching style

A predictable teaching style using a **limited repertoire** of techniques is sure to bore your students. Provide variety and you will see an increase in their motivation. Use the checklist of techniques to determine how varied your teaching style is – introduce more variety when you have done this!

We are all lifelong learners and we can always learn a new teaching technique.

Over the last half-term have your students (*tick where appropriate*):

Used a newspaper?	❏	Done individual or group research?	❏
Played a game?	❏	Undertaken extended reading?	❏
Answered questions from a book?	❏	Had a brainstorming session?	❏
Had a discussion?	❏	Drawn a graph or used statistics?	❏
Made a model?	❏	Drawn a diagram or cartoon?	❏
Done a quiz or test?	❏	Used music in their work?	❏
Written an essay	❏	Been *outdoors* for a task or activity?	❏
Written a newspaper article?	❏	Worked with an outside speaker?	❏
Worked in a pair or a group?	❏	Sat in different places from usual?	❏
Had a debate?	❏	Worked in the school library?	❏
Role-played?	❏	Worked on a poster?	❏
Made up a play or a TV/radio script?	❏	Worked with somebody they don't know well?	❏

Teaching your students how to learn

There is now much emphasis placed on acquiring the knowledge and skills to learn effectively. The work of organisations like the Campaign for Learning (www.campaign-for-learning.org.uk) have put these **learning skills** on the educational map, and the government has recently signalled its intention to promote them. (See also the *Learning to Learn Pocketbook*.)

You can promote learning skills in your classroom by:

- Teaching your students about their **brains**, **learning** and **memory**
- Emphasising the importance of **study techniques** such as mind mapping and memory systems
- Encouraging your students to find out about their **preferred learning styles** and main **intelligences**
- **Modelling** good practice in your own work

The only educated man is the one who has learned how to learn
Arthur C. Clarke

Using music to aid learning

Music can be used in a variety of ways to promote learning. Many research studies have shown the beneficial effects of music on learning, and some have linked certain types of music with enhanced performance in tests (the *Mozart effect*).

- Ask for a show of hands on how many **students listen to music while they work at home** – you will be hard pushed to find any who prefer silence
- This is often in **sharp contrast** to the preferences of teachers, especially those well in to their careers
- Allowing music to be played in lessons is still a **big step** for many teachers, but if managed carefully can be a valuable tool
- Using music is certainly **not** simply a matter of turning the radio on – there is a whole science behind its use to aid learning

Because music can both calm and stimulate, it offers one of the quickest ways to influence the mood of a group
Jeanette Vos

Using music to aid learning

Things to consider when using music in the classroom:

- The **teacher** should decide when it is appropriate to play music
- Use different **tempos** for different parts of the lesson, eg upbeat music as students enter, atmospheric music to set the scene, calming music for students to work to, evocative music for a review
- Music with about **60 beats** per minute is widely considered to be best for helping students concentrate on specific tasks (because it equates to the resting heartbeat)
- Music of heartbeat tempo has a **calming** effect but can also stimulate **alpha waves** in the brain which create a state of relaxed alertness
- Modern **pop** and **classical** music are now considered equally helpful in aiding learning; it is simply a matter of how the music is used
- **Negotiate** with your students as to the kind of music that should be played, pointing out there is a science behind using music and it is not just a treat

Health and safety issues

Good practice with regard to **health and safety** issues should be central to your work as teacher.

- The degree of risk to students will depend very much on the subject you teach
- A chemistry laboratory is obviously a riskier place in which to teach than an English classroom, but there are many hidden risks in even the most innocuous setting
- Your school is required to have a rigorous health and safety policy, and departmental policy statements are also important
- Encourage your students to regard respect for health and safety as an essential part of classroom practice

Setting and streaming

There are no hard and fast rules on what works best in **setting or streaming** groups.

- In most cases this will be a decision for middle and senior management and you will be presented with a class which is either of mixed-ability or grouped according to ability

- Educationally, the jury is still out on whether grouping students by ability produces better results, though in some schools one approach is enshrined in the culture as the best arrangement

- Adapting your teaching to take account of the ability profile of the group is paramount

Target setting

All your students should have clear **targets** in your subject area. The greater their involvement in setting these targets, the better the chance they will meet them.

There are various types of targets which are applicable:

- A target grade in a GCSE or other formal examination
- A target mark in the next test
- A target grade in a particular piece of work
- A student's individual learning targets on a piece of work

A convenient way to record these targets is the *student subject record card* which is kept and completed by the student, and is the place to record other key details about individual progress (see next page).

It is important to **review** the progress
your students have made towards
their targets at regular intervals,
and to set new and challenging ones.

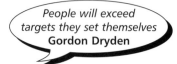

People will exceed targets they set themselves
Gordon Dryden

The student subject record

This provides a single reference point for the student, their teacher(s) and parents/carers.

STUDENT PROGRESS BOOKLET

What is the purpose of this booklet?

Marks gained

Tests and examinations

GCSE course work

Other achievements

Reviews and targets

Reports

Personal targets

Assessment

Assessment is used to appraise students' performance. It provides:

- Feedback about student progress to you and the student
- A statement of current attainment
- A written record of progress over time
- An assessment of students' readiness for future learning
- Evidence about your effectiveness as a teacher

There are several **types** of assessment, most of which are classified as formative or summative:

- **Formative** assessment – designed to promote effective future learning by identifying difficulties, errors or misunderstandings and offering guidance to improve
- **Summative** assessment – designed to identify the standard attainment at a particular time and usually carried out at the end of a period of instruction, resulting in a grade or level

Adapted from Kyriacou (1998)

Assessment

Use assessment to help students make progress:

- Have a **variety** of forms of assessment, from short tests to lengthy written assignments
- Let your students know **why** and **when** they are taking each assessment
- Teach **revision skills** to prepare your students for assessments
- Carry out a **baseline assessment** at the beginning of each year
- Use baseline assessment data to **predict** future performance and **monitor** progress
- Keep **portfolios** of students' work at different levels
- Always explain to students how their performance in assessments can be **improved** to reach the next level
- Do **not** let teaching towards National Curriculum and other external tests dominate your lessons too much

The government's renewed emphasis on Assessment for Learning is encouraging teachers to use formative assessment as a means of helping all students to achieve their potential.

Marking

Effective **marking** takes time, but it can have a profound impact on the learner. Marking is effective when:

- It gives a clear indication of the **level/grade** reached
- It is **developmental** – ie indicates how the work needs to be improved to reach the next level/grade
- It helps the learner improve their **literacy** as well as competence within the subject area (give simple codes for spelling, grammar and punctuation mistakes)
- It includes **supportive comments** about the learner's work
- It is supplemented from time to time with **verbal comment** and encouragement on a one-to-one basis

It is not necessary to mark every aspect of a student's work each time you look at their book. Instead, consider focusing on a specific aspect of their performance to make the feedback more targeted and more manageable at the same time.

Always provide consistent feedback when marking.

Homework

Homework should be used to extend learning beyond the classroom. Although not always popular with students, it can provide the opportunity for a range of tasks to be carried out which cannot be done in school time. For many subjects it is a means of completing overfull examination syllabuses.

Homework is **effective** when:

- It is used to extend and enrich learning
- It builds on what has been learnt in the lesson
- It takes advantages of the opportunities in the students' home lives, eg parents/carers, grandparents, local features of interest
- It is enjoyable

Homework should **not** be:

- Simply finishing off work done in lessons
- Optional
- Given only to those who work hard
- Given only to those who do not finish a piece of work in class

Celebrating achievements

Take every opportunity to **celebrate the achievements** and successes of your students.

- Give copious written and verbal **praise** – students thrive on it
- **Display** students' work prominently on your classroom walls and in corridor displays
- **Include reports** on students' work – or extracts from the work itself – in the school newsletter/magazine
- Try to get coverage in your **local newspaper** of particularly noteworthy achievements
- Enter your students' work for **competitions**
- Have a well earned **celebration** at the end of each term – a Christmas party, quiz or event

Ask your students how to improve

Your **students** are an invaluable source of information that will help you **improve your teaching**. Ask them frequently for their comments, both verbally and via written questionnaires.

- Young people usually give **honest**, **fair and helpful** answers when given the opportunity to comment on the quality of teaching
- If you can have an **open relationship** about the quality of your own performance, then it is much easier to be critical and give advice to your students about theirs
- Cultivate an atmosphere where everyone in the classroom is learning and needs help to do so, **including** you as the teacher
- Adopting this approach requires faith, a willingness to **accept criticism** and **take risks** – but it will make you stronger and better as a teacher

Ask your students how to improve

I need your views to help me become a better teacher. Please complete this sheet as fully and honestly as you can. You do not have to put your name on this sheet.

1. Over the last half-term (or unit of work) how much do you think you have learnt from my lessons?

   1, 2, 3, 4, 5, 6, 7, 8, 9, 10
   (circle the number that applies best, where 1 = very little and 10 = very much)

2. Over the last half-term how much have you enjoyed my lessons?

   1, 2, 3, 4, 5, 6, 7, 8, 9, 10

3. What do you enjoy about my lessons?

4. What do you not enjoy about my lessons?

5. Mention three things that I could do that would make me a better teacher.

Thank you very much for your help

Example questionnaire to students on the quality of teaching

The advantage of using a scale on some of the questions is that it generates quantitative data which can be analysed and graphed. After an initial questionnaire such as this has been used, a much more sophisticated one can be devised to ask about particular aspects of your teaching in the future.

Student review meetings

Opportunities to meet parents/carers **alongside** students are extremely valuable.

Student review meetings should:

- **Always** take place with the student present
- Last at least **five minutes**
- Contain periods when the **student is talking** about their own learning
- Be focused on the student's **current level** of achievement and effort and what they can do to **improve**
- Include opportunities for parents/carers to ask **questions**
- Finish with a brief **action plan** for the student for the next few months, that includes what the student, teacher and parent/carer need to do

Student review meetings

Students can prepare for their review meetings by completing a **prompt sheet**. This will be used by the student during the meeting to comment on their progress. It is vital that students are given such opportunities to be reflective about their progress.

Students should prepare written answers on the prompt sheet in a lesson leading up to the review evening. You should discuss this with each student to ensure the responses are realistic.

1. What level/standard have you reached in this subject this year?

_____

2. What have you enjoyed learning about?

_____

3. What have you not enjoyed learning about?

_____

4. How hard have you tried? (use a scale of 1-10 to indicate effort, where 10 = maximum effort)

_____

5. What have your strengths in this subject been this year?

_____

6. What have your weaknesses in this subject been this year?

_____

7. What is your target grade/level for next term?

_____

8. What do you need to do to reach that grade?

_____

9. Write a mini action plan for what you will try to do over the next term to improve your work.

_____

10. What can your teacher and parents/carers do to help you reach your potential?

Maintaining good student relationships

If you teach well and show you are interested in the progress of your students they will respect you. However, some specific actions will help maintain **excellent working relationships**:

- Ask students for their **views** whenever possible – this empowers them and underlines that their opinions are valued and respected
- Show you **care** and are **interested** in the home lives of your students by asking about what they have been doing outside school – try to bring their personal experiences into the classroom
- Reveal a little about your **own life** outside school and the things you like to do – this will make you more human in their eyes!

Remember the **most effective learning takes** place where there are strong working relationships between the teacher and the students, based on trust and mutual respect.

Learning outside the classroom

Students enjoy the chance to learn **outside** the classroom on excursions, field visits and residentials. Some subjects lend themselves better to such enrichment activities than others, but you should find at least one opportunity with each class every term to take the learning beyond the classroom.

Examples include:

- A poetry reading
- A theatre visit
- A maths challenge
- A geography field trip
- A visit to a museum
- An athletics event

Asking your students to write a report on the visit can be a valuable educational exercise too.

Learning outside the classroom

Questions to consider in planning excursions, field visits and residentials:

- What are the learning objectives?
- How will the visit enhance the curriculum?
- What is the staff/student ratio?
- Has the activity been risk assessed?
- What information needs to go in the letter to parents/carers?
- What links will there be to other aspects of the curriculum?
- What is the cost and suggested parental contribution?

And after the experience:

- How successful was it?
- What were the students' views?

Ofsted inspections

Every teacher has to get used to the periodic visits of Ofsted **inspectors** who make judgements on the quality of teaching and learning.

- Try to act **naturally** and teach the way you normally do (it should be good enough without putting on a show)
- Write careful **lesson plans** which are made available to the inspectors but do not over-prepare your lessons
- Focus on the quality of **learning** that is taking place in your classroom
- Always take a **register** at the start of the lesson
- Following the **accelerated learning** sequence outlined on pages 18-19 as you deliver lessons
- Be prepared to stand up for your own **professional judgement** if challenged by an inspector – you know your students better than the inspector does
- **Study the Ofsted report** carefully to see what you can do better

Ofsted inspections

Ofsted inspectors should be able to answer **yes** to the following questions after observing your lessons:

- Were the learning objectives of the lesson clear?
- Was the lesson purposeful, with high expectations of students?
- Did the lesson engage students' interest?
- Was the work matched to students' abilities and learning needs?
- Were pupils given opportunities to make choices and organise their own work?
- Were appropriate questioning strategies used to develop students' language and thinking?
- Were a variety of learning activities used?
- Was the behaviour of students good and were any incidents of inappropriate behaviour dealt with promptly and sensitively?
- Did the lesson have a clear structure and maintain good pace throughout?
- Was the teaching effective overall?
- Did all students make progress and learn something new?

Information & communication technology

Information and communication technology (ICT) is an important tool for promoting learning. Its various forms should be incorporated regularly into lessons, through:

- Use of computers
- Access to the internet
- Use of digital still and video cameras
- Subject-specific ICT equipment, eg computer aided design and manufacture

Remember that using the technology is not an end in itself – the key issue is the impact it has on **learning** and the development of **ICT skills**.

Enrichment opportunities

Organise on-site **enrichment** activities based around your subject area, during and outside school hours. Students will appreciate the opportunities they provide and such activities can have a positive effect on their levels of motivation.

Examples include:

- An outside speaker
- A specialist workshop or masterclass
- A community group working with a class
- A theatre presentation to a year group
- An expert working with a club
- A question and answer session with a local business

Be clear about the **educational value** of all such enrichment activities and try to verify the quality before making any bookings.

Clubs

A regular subject-based **club** can provide opportunities to extend learning beyond the classroom. Clubs can also allow the time to explore some of the more fun aspects of the subject, outside the constraints of the National Curriculum.

Clubs are effective where they:

- Are open to **all**
- Comprise a **committed** group of students
- Have clearly stated **aims** that are negotiated with the club members
- Allow opportunities for **students** to take the lead
- Provide **cross-curricular** opportunities
- Encompass **citizenship** issues
- Are fun!

Preparing
to Teach

 The Craft
of Teaching

 Other Aspects
of the Role

 Progressing in
Your Career

 Reference
Section

 Further
Information

Other Aspects
of the Role

The role of the form tutor

In common with most teachers in secondary schools, you will probably also fulfil an important additional role as a **form tutor**. Form tutors:

- Take the register during morning and afternoon registration for a particular class
- Administer general school notices and relay essential information to students, and through them to their parents/carers
- Are an immediate point of contact for students in their form group on pastoral matters
- Help students in their form group make academic and personal progress through target-setting and other monitoring strategies
- In some schools teach personal, social and health education to their form group

In many secondary schools the form tutor will stay with a class as they move up through the school. In others the class has a different form tutor each year.

Becoming a more effective form tutor

1. **Establish clear rules and expectations** for behaviour during registration, and model the kind of behaviour you expect
2. **Celebrate the achievements** of individual students and groups within and outside school
3. **Listen** to the views of your students on school and non-school issues
4. **Be available to give extra individual help**, and let your form group know when these times are
5. **Organise a regular form group outing** (eg bowling alley, theatre) to maintain a group identity and develop social skills
6. Insist that every student in your form group participates in **at least** one extra-curricular activity
7. Encourage students in your form group to make new friends by organising quick games and activities, or asking them to sit next to a different student every half-term
8. **Use *dead* time** during registration for brain games, puzzles and group discussion
9. **Encourage quiet reflection** by having a thought for the day
10. **Take care of your appearance** and dress smartly!

Raising the profile of your subject

It is important that you try to **raise the profile** of your subject and find ways to demonstrate its value. If yours is an option subject this may well be necessary to ensure you have sufficient numbers to keep you in a job!

- Get students to **write articles** in the school magazine/newsletter about what they have been doing in the subject
- **Issue press releases** to local newspapers about special projects, trips and achievements
- Make a subject-based **display** with engaging photographs and examples of students' work and put this in the entrance area to the school
- Find opportunities for your students' work to be displayed in the **community**, eg in the local supermarket or library
- Do not miss **special days or weeks** linked to your subject, eg National Spring Clean Week, maths day, poetry week

Fundraising

Many teachers are now successful at bringing in **extra income** for their departments, which allows additional resources to be purchased. Your school may have a member of staff responsible for fundraising. Consider the following possible sources of funds:

- The National Lottery
- Competitions and awards
- Grant-making trusts
- Local businesses
- School events
- Special projects, eg running a fair trade shop

Discuss your resource needs with your head of department and **prepare a fundraising strategy** that will improve resources for all.

Meetings

Meetings will be a regular feature in your diary. Thankfully in most schools they are now much more focused than in the past, with a clear agenda, timescale and an obvious link to how students' learning can be improved.

To get the most out of meetings:

- Read the **agenda** before the meeting, noting down points you want to contribute
- Record **action points** that you need to carry forward, as well as noting those actions you will need to influence
- Keep reminding yourself that the purpose of every meeting in school is fundamentally about improving **opportunities** for your students
- Offer to **chair** meetings from time to time, especially in topics you feel especially passionate about

Managing stress

Teaching is widely recognised as one of the most **stressful** professions. If your levels of stress are having a negative impact on your quality of life then it is time to do something about it.

Twelve ways to reduce your stress levels:

1 Learn to **recognise** stress and act **early** to reduce it

2 Realise that you **can** do something to reduce your levels of stress and feel healthier

3 Be **tidy** and **organised** to help you deal with the demands on you

4 Try to identify the **triggers** for stress and find ways to minimise their effect

5 **Pace** yourself by taking regular breaks when you mark and plan lessons

6 **Learn to say *no*** to additional work you cannot take on

7 Practise **switching off** from school work for at least one day at the weekend – it is a skill that **does** become easier to do if you work at it

Managing stress (cont'd)

8   Do not skimp on **exercise**, **sleep** or **holidays**

9   **Eat healthily** avoid too much fat and sugar and try to stay clear of high caffeine drinks and other stimulants

10 Try **relaxation**, **yoga** or **meditation** classes

11 Realise that if you are **trying your best** for your students then this is good enough – you have not signed up to a life without weekends or a social life

12 Realise when it's time to **ask for help** when you are struggling in your work

Managing your time

Developing good **time management** skills is crucial to being effective in school, while maintaining a satisfactory home-work balance. Your time management skills should improve as you get used to the role, but remember the following:

- Be aware of how you use your time by keeping a **weekly log**
- Use a planner to rigorously **schedule** all work
- Keep a master **'to do'** list that is frequently reviewed
- Include **thinking** and **planning** time in your weekly schedule
- Find your **best time of day** to carry out particular tasks and stick to them
- **Empty your pigeon hole daily**, being ruthless with items you do not need to keep
- Always **prioritise** tasks
- Do not prepare your lessons in **minute** detail – some of the best lessons evolve from a basic plan that need not take hours to produce
- Use **admin staff** effectively
- Understand that your work will **never** seem finished; fix a time when you will finish working on a task and keep to it

Holidays

You will probably be used to the familiar comments from non-teaching friends about the outrageous length of teachers' **holidays**. Only teachers know how many of the supposed days off are taken up by marking, preparation, stocktaking and other administrative duties.

Although half-term holidays can be a good time to catch up on these tasks, the relentless pace of work during term time will mean that many teachers use their holidays to catch up on sleep!

Have some **ground rules for your holidays** to avoid them being eroded, eg

- Make sure you devote at least two days of your half term-break to relaxation – you deserve it
- Devote at least a week of the Christmas break to your family and friends
- At Easter and during the summer break try to get away from home for at least a week

Switching off from school work will make you more effective once term begins – we all need a break to keep us creative.

Preparing
to Teach

 The Craft
of Teaching

 Other Aspects
of the Role

 Progressing in
Your Career

 Reference
Section

 Further
Information

Progressing in
Your Career

Continuing Professional Development

It is important to take an interest in your own **professional development**.
There are many excellent courses which you can attend that will make you a better
teacher and improve your performance in the classroom.

- Agree at least one professional development
  target as part of your annual review with your
  line manager
- Keep a look out for courses that are of
  interest throughout the year
- Make sure you follow up every course you
  attend with some time to put in place the
  things you have learnt
- Keep an up-to-date professional
  development file with copies of
  certificates (this can be taken to
  interviews)

Performance management

Every teacher undergoes a formal appraisal each year which is termed **performance management**. This takes place during an interview with your line manager during which personal objectives are set.

- Be as open as possible during your appraisal, making sure you have given yourself time to think things through before going into the meeting
- Include at least one objective about student performance, based on quantitative (number) data
- Include an objective linked to your professional development
- Be sure to set SMART objectives (Specific, Measurable, Achievable, Relevant, Time-related)
- Keep your copy of the appraisal statement for future reference

Remember that as well as being an opportunity to review how well you are doing, performance management is your chance to identify ways in which other staff can support you, and the training you would like. **Use it!**

Going through the threshold

In England, on reaching scale point M6 on the teacher's pay scale, you are entitled to apply to go through the first stage of the **threshold**, giving you additional pay and access to a higher pay scale. You will have to fill in an application form that is considered by an external assessor.

Advice on applying to go through the threshold:

- Spend some time gathering the **data** that will be needed for your application
- Complete the application form **carefully**, like you would a job application form
- Make your **achievements** while in post clear
- Seek the **assistance** of colleagues who have already gone through the threshold, but avoid model answers
- Give yourself plenty of **time** to complete the form
- If you are not successful discuss the matter with your union representative

There are two further upper threshold levels which are possible, but these are undergoing review by the government, with the requirements becoming more stringent.

Finding a new job

The *Times Educational Supplement* frequently bulges under the weight of hundreds of pages of **adverts** for teachers. Some weeks there are over 3,000 education vacancies of one sort or another. It is much easier to find jobs in some subjects (science, maths, languages) than in others (drama, art, PE), but there are still plenty of jobs to apply for most weeks.

- There are no set rules for when it is the right time to move on – it depends on how ambitious you are and what your ultimate aim is
- Do not base your decision to leave post on the bust-up with 11Z on a Friday afternoon! It happens to every teacher
- Take advice from trusted colleagues on when you are ready to move upward
- Send for plenty of job details to get a feel for the kind of qualities and experience that employers are looking for
- If you are moving into middle management, be prepared for the extra **leadership** and **managerial** duties that you will have to take on in addition to your teaching duties

Job application forms

Most schools now issue standard **applications forms** from their local authority which you need to return with a letter of application. These are obtained by telephoning the school, or increasingly from school websites.

Guidelines for job application forms:

- Make sure you **complete all sections** as requested
- Study carefully the **job and person specification**
- **Match** as closely as you can your application to what the employer is looking for
- **Write concisely** and use bold and bullet points to structure your responses
- **The most important section is the open-ended one** about how your qualifications, skills and experience make you a suitable candidate – spend the most time on this
- **Draft your responses out** before committing them to paper (use a word processor and cut and paste if this is permitted or write very neatly in black ink)
- **Do not send extra material unless it is asked for** – this can sometimes disqualify you from being considered
- Check for **accuracy**
- Always **tell the truth**

The letter of application

The **letter of application** may accompany an application form or a curriculum vitae. It provides the opportunity to outline how your qualifications, skills and experience match the application, where this has not been possible in the application form itself.

Guidelines for the letter of application:

- Try to keep the letter **concise** and to the point (500 words maximum)
- Be positive about your achievements but **do not exaggerate** and **never lie**
- **Check spelling and grammar very carefully** (better still get someone else to proof-read your letter)
- **Do not use personal pleas**, eg *'I have always wanted to work in X area and would be really disappointed if I were not offered an interview'*
- **Make your letter stand out from the crowd** through its quality, completeness or your unique achievements
- **Give yourself plenty of time** to meet the deadline for returning your application

Your curriculum vitae

Not many schools will ask for your **curriculum vitae** these days as the local authority application form/letter of application is preferred. Nevertheless, a CV is a good place to summarise your career and personal details so they can be transferred onto application forms.

Suggested content for your CV:

Name

Personal profile	A summary of your qualities and the type of work you are seeking
Job history	Include all relevant work, even if not in teaching
Qualifications	GCSEs, A-levels, degrees, plus other public exams and any professional qualifications
Skills	List these with evidence
Achievements	Bullet point your major achievements in your current post
Personal details	Your contact details; date of birth
Referees	Addresses of two people who can confirm your suitability for employment; one must be your current employer

Curriculum Vitae

Name

Personal profile

Job history

Qualifications

Skills

Achievements

Personal details

Referees

BROMPTON SECONDARY SCHOOL
BEANLEY LANE
WINCHESTER
HAMPSHIRE
SO22 3GB

Interviews

You will be notified by letter (and sometimes also by phone) if you have been shortlisted for **interview**. Schools like to shortlist about 4-6 candidates to give them a reasonable field to draw from.

Before the interview day:

- **Read a summary of the school's latest Ofsted inspection report** (www.ofsted.gov.uk) to give you an insight into the school
- **Practise answers to commonly-asked interview** questions (eg: *Why do you want this job? What skills would you bring to the role? Where do you see yourself in five years' time?*)
- **Prepare a couple of questions of your own** to ask during the interview
- **Get a good night's sleep** the night before

Interviews

On the **interview day**:

- Make sure you **give yourself plenty of time** to get to the school (arriving late creates a poor impression)
- **Dress smartly and try to smile and be positive**, without being creepy
- Take your **up-to-date professional development file** with you
- **Take a sheet into the interview with your prepared questions on** and also some prompts for the kind of messages you want to put across – brief bullet points or symbols
- Answer the panel's questions **fully and honestly**
- If you do not understand the question **ask for it to be repeated**
- If you cannot answer the question ask to **move on to the next one**
- **Do not ramble** – stop when you have said what you need to
- It is acceptable to have a little **thinking time** if you are asked a tricky question
- Be prepared to **answer honestly** the question: *If you were offered the post today would you take it?*

Interviews

After the interview:

If you are successful

- You will usually be offered the post there and then
- **Agree a date** when you can go and visit the school again before you start teaching there
- Take away any **details of the school** (eg prospectus, staff handbook) that will help you settle in

If you do not get the job

- You should be offered a **de-brief** with a senior member of staff (most likely the head teacher) – take this opportunity to learn what the school thought your strengths and weaknesses were
- **Write down the interview questions** – they will help you prepare for the next one
- **Don't be bitter** about not getting the job – it is the school's loss

Preparing
to Teach

The Craft
of Teaching

Other Aspects
of the Role

Progressing in
Your Career

Reference
Section

Further
Information

Reference Section

Governors

Your **governing** body has ultimate responsibility for the running of the school, although your head teacher will most likely take many of the key day-to-day decisions, calling on governors for advice where appropriate.

- Governors have an important role in hiring and firing staff, and will be regular visitors to your school when interviews are held
- They bring a wealth of expertise and experience to their roles and if your governing body is strong, your school is likely to be successful
- All governors are unpaid for their valuable work and should be cherished by staff and students – in reality many staff and students rarely come into contact with governors and the hard work of these sterling volunteers goes unrecognised

Governors may sometimes come and observe you teach. Make a point of welcoming them into your classroom.

The staff handbook

Your school should issue an annual **staff handbook** in September setting out all the key information you need to know about the school and the academic year ahead. It will include:

- Your school's mission statement
- An explanation of staff roles
- Information on sanctions and rewards
- Copies of school policies
- Details of school procedures, eg uniform, excursions
- The school calendar

Read your school handbook at the start of every year – it contains valuable information.

School policies

Schools should have a range of written **policies** in place that deal with key issues, which may include:

- Behaviour
- Child protection
- Sex education
- Curriculum and assessment
- Partnership with parents and the community
- Bullying

- Teaching and learning
- Pastoral care
- Inclusion
- Multi-cultural education
- Health and safety
- Race equality

These policies should be:

- Easily accessible
- Open to public scrutiny
- Concise and easy to read
- Written with the full consultation of staff and governors

- Subject to annual review
- Flexible to take account of changing circumstances

Make school policies a continual reference point for your work.

Development plans

Your school will have a detailed **development plan** or improvement plan charting priorities over the coming three to four years. It will:

- Be focused on raising student achievement
- Include as headings: Targets, Activity, Timescale, Costs, Success outcomes, Monitoring strategies, Person(s) responsible
- Include SMART targets (Specific, Measurable, Achievable, Relevant, Time-related)
- Be agreed in consultation with staff
- Be used by heads of department to help prepare subject development plans

Keep the development plan to hand and use it as the foundation for your work.

Pastoral care in schools

Studies have shown that students perform better in schools that have effective **pastoral** support. Pastoral care is effective if:

- Students enjoy coming to school and want to learn
- Relationships between students and staff are good
- Support outside the classroom is provided for students experiencing difficulties
- Instances of bullying or other oppressive behaviour are dealt with promptly and fairly
- Students are treated as individuals
- Staff are prepared to be flexible about the needs of individual students

Play your part in developing an effective pastoral care system in your school.

Teacher induction

If you are a **newly qualified teacher** you are entitled to a special package of support to help you settle into your new role. It should include:

- A reduced timetable to help with lesson preparation
- A school induction tutor to observe you teach and advise on teaching and learning strategies
- Opportunities to observe experienced colleagues teach
- Extra professional development opportunities

If you are a teacher new to a school you may be given a mentor to ease your transition, but you are unlikely to be offered a reduced timetable.

Make the most of your induction package.

The National Curriculum

The **National Curriculum** for England sets out the knowledge, skills and understanding that underpins the education of children age 5-16 in the maintained sector. It is legally binding for schools, and is organised on the basis of four **key stages**, with a number of compulsory subjects at each key stage (see dots in table).

Schools are also required to provide **religious and sex education**, although parents/carers can chose to withdraw their children from these lessons. **Careers education** during years 9, 10 and 11 must also be provided.

The National Curriculum

	Key stage 1	Key stage 2	Key stage 3	Key stage 4	National Curriculum core subjects	National Curriculum non-core foundation subjects
Age	5-7	7-11	11-14	14-16		
Year groups	1-2	3-6	7-9	10-11		
English	•	•	•	•	•	
Mathematics	•	•	•	•	•	
Science	•	•	•	•	•	
Design & technology	•	•	•			•
Information & communication technology	•	•	•	•	•	
History	•	•	•			•
Geography	•	•	•			•
Modern foreign languages			•			•
Art & design	•	•	•			•
Music	•	•	•			•
Physical education	•	•	•	•		•
Citizenship			•	•		•

Based on The National Curriculum

Learning across the National Curriculum

In addition to the twelve distinct subjects within the National Curriculum, your school must also provide opportunities for *learning across the curriculum*, including:

- **Spiritual** development
- **Moral** development
- **Social** development
- **Cultural** development

The government provides a non-statutory framework for developing the above, through **personal, social and health education**. Most schools have separate lessons dealing with this dimension, which are sometimes combined with citizenship or careers in PSHCE (personal, social, health and citizenship or careers education).

Key skills in the National Curriculum

Your school is also required to promote more general skills, particularly six **key skills** that are embedded in the National Curriculum:

- Communication
- Application of number
- Information technology
- Working with others
- Improving own learning and performance
- Problem-solving

These skill areas are described as key skills because they help learners to improve their learning and equip them for education, work and life in general.

Thinking skills in the National Curriculum

The following five **thinking skills** are embedded in the National Curriculum:

- Information-processing skills
- Reasoning skills
- Enquiry skills

- Creative thinking skills
- Evaluation skills

While using these skills students focus on *knowing how*, as well as *knowing what* – in this way they learn how to learn. Teaching Thinking is having a profound impact in many schools and is now the focus of several government and non-government programmes.

Bloom's taxonomy of cognitive development provides a helpful framework of how to move your students towards **higher order** thinking skills.

Bloom's Taxonomy

Other aspects of the school curriculum

Your school must also build the following **four additional themes** into the curriculum:

- Financial capability
- Enterprise and entrepreneurial skills
- Work-related learning
- Education for sustainable development

As a result of the raft of compulsory and recommended elements of the school curriculum, your students will sometimes feel like they are on an educational treadmill. England has one of the most crowded and prescriptive curricula of any country worldwide, though the revised National Curriculum for key stages 3-4 (see next page) signals a much more flexible approach for schools.

Studies usually reveal, however, that **young people are generally content with their education and enjoy attending school**. Their resilience is impressive!

The revised Key Stage 3/4 Curriculum

From September 2008 the government is moving to a much less prescriptive curriculum model for schools. This will allow flexibility to study different aspects of the curriculum, and will see reductions to the content that must be taught in years 7-11.

The revised curriculum will also see renewed emphasis on seven key 'cross-curricular dimensions', some of which build on the areas highlighted previously. They are:

- Identity and cultural diversity
- Healthy lifestyles
- Community participation
- Enterprise
- Global dimension and sustainable development
- Technology and the media
- Creativity and critical thinking

Although these dimensions are not statutory, schools will find them useful in designing and planning their wider curriculum, helping them to personalise learning. Details of the revised National Curriculum can be found at www.qca.org.uk

The Key Stage 3 Strategy

The government's **Key Stage 3 National Strategy** continues to exert a strong influence in schools, with fresh priorities being regularly introduced. It aims to raise standards by strengthening teaching and learning across the curriculum for all students aged 11 to 14, in particular in English, mathematics, science and ICT. There is also a strand linked to the foundation subjects.

This major initiative builds on the success of the National Literacy and National Numeracy Strategies in primary schools and is based on:

- **High expectations** and challenging targets for all pupils
- Strengthening **progression** from Key Stage 2 to Key Stage 3
- Promoting teaching strategies that **engage** students in their learning
- **Professional development** and support to bring about change

If you teach one of the core subjects you will already have had to rethink your practice with students in years 7-9. If you teach a foundation subject **keep an eye on developments** in your subject and be prepared to get involved in any pilots. New areas of emphasis are being announced all the time.

Further Information: books

Accelerated Learning in Practice by Alistair Smith
Published by Network Educational Press, 1998

Effective teaching in schools by Chris Kyriacou
Published by Nelson Thornes, 1997

Essential teaching skills by Chris Kyriacou
Published by Nelson Thornes, 1998

How to improve your school: giving pupils a voice by Jean Ruddock and Julia Flutter
Published by Continuum, 2004

Learning to teach in the secondary school: a companion to school experience
by Susan Capel, Marilyn Leask and Tony Turner
Published by Routledge, 1999

The National Curriculum: handbook for secondary teachers in England
Published by The Stationery Office, 1999

And from the Teachers' Pocketbooks series:

- *Managing Workload*
- *Behaviour Management*
- *Form Tutor's*

- *Creative Teaching*
- *Inclusion*
- *Jobs & Interviews*

- *Learning to Learn*
- *Assessment & Learning*
- *Teaching Thinking*

Further information: websites

Professional Associations

www.teachers.org.uk — National Union of Teachers

www.nasuwt.org.uk — National Association of Schoolmasters Union of Women Teachers

www.askatl.org.uk — Association of Teachers and Lecturers

Government

www.nc.uk.net — National Curriculum online

www.dcsf.gov.uk — The Department of Children, Schools and Families

www.teachernet.gov.uk — The UK government gateway for educational professionals

Education portals

www.schoolzone.co.uk — The UK's biggest and most-used education portal site

www.schoolsnet.com — The second largest education portal site

About the author

Brin Best BSc, PGCE, FRGS, FMA is a consultant specialising in school improvement and classroom change. He formed Innovation *for* Education Ltd in 2002 to help teachers and school leaders create a brighter future for young people. He has carried out a wide range of roles within education, including classroom teacher, head of department, school development officer and local authority advisory teacher. He writes and speaks widely on education issues and is the author of a dozen books aimed at education professionals. He is also carrying out part-time doctoral research at Leeds University into effective teaching and learning approaches. Whilst a teacher, his department and students received numerous awards and in 2000 he received a Millennium Fellowship for his pioneering work on environmental education. Brin is also series consultant for Teachers' Pocketbooks.

He can be contacted at: Innovation *for* Education Ltd, 9 Throstle Nest Close, Otley, West Yorkshire LS21 2RR
Tel. +44 (0) 1943 466500 Email brinbest@hotmail.com

Acknowledgements
I am very grateful to my ex-colleagues and students at Settle High School and Community College where I learnt the craft of teaching. Many thanks also to Elaine Doxey for providing valuable input to the pages on inclusion.